Love.....
Saves:
The Endangered Species

by Bradley Zink

ISBN-10: 1512241385
ISBN-13: 978-1512241389

DEDICATION

I would like to dedicated this book to ALL of the people out there that are doing their part to help protect the endangered species of the world.

Without their tireless efforts, we would not be able to enjoy these majestic animals of our glorious planet. Without their dedication, these animals would have no hope. Without their vision, our future generations would never know of these Endangered Species

CONTENTS

ACKNOWLEDGMENTS

I would like to thank the NSEFU Wildlife Conservation Foundation for honoring me to write this book for them, and bring to everyone the message to "Preserve and Protect our Endangered Species".

I would also like to thank everyone for all the hard work and devotion that goes into the conservation efforts. With the ongoing efforts, and support of organizations like the San Diego Zoo and Safari Park, the public is able to enjoy the beauty of these amazing animals.

American Bald Eagle

American Bald Eagle
(Haliaeetus leucocephalus)

Endangered Status: Threatened

The bald eagle is both the national bird and national animal of the United States of America.

In the late 20th century it was on the brink of extirpation in the contiguous United States. Populations have since recovered and the species was removed from the U.S. government's list of endangered species on July 12, 1995

Fun Fact: Bald Eagles are master nest builders. The largest known nest measured 9 feet across, 20 feet deep and weighed more than 2 tons

Sudan Red-fronted Gazelle

Sudan Red-fronted Gazelle
(Eudorcas rufifrons)

Endangered Status: Vulnerable

Approximately 15% of the total population of this species occurs in protected areas

Red-fronted Gazelle populations have been reduced to scattered remnants over most of its range by illegal hunting, competition with domestic livestock and habitat degradation. It is likely to be extinct in Ghana.

Fun Fact: When alarmed, this species produces a series of short "wheezy snorts" while pinching the nostrils forward

Southern White Rhinoceros

Southern White Rhinoceros (Ceratotherium simum)

Endangered Status: Threatened

The Southern White Rhino's survival portrays one of conservation's success stories.

In the late 19th century it was on the brink of extinction, with less than 100 left. Populations have since recovered and the species now numbers more than 14,000. Poaching and hunting still are a constant threat, though.

Fun Fact: Despite its size, white rhinos can reach speeds of up to 28 miles per hour

Southern Gerenuk

Southern Gerenuk
(Litocranius walleri)

Endangered Status: Threatened

The gerenuk is a graceful creature with a long, thin neck. This feature inspired the name "gerenuk", which means "giraffe-necked" in the Somali language.

Although habitat loss has contributed to the Gerenuk's decline, the largest threats to the creatures are from predators and hunters.

Fun Fact: The gerenuk is exceptionally well adapted to arid conditions and does not drink free water. It obtains all the water it needs from eating grasses and leaves.

East African Bongo Antelope

East African Bongo Antelope (Tragelaphus eurycerus)

Endangered Status: Critically Endangered

The bongo faces an ongoing population decline as habitat destruction and meat hunting pressures increase with the relentless expansion of human settlement.

The eastern mountain bongo has never been plentiful. Historically, hunting, poaching, and lion predation decimated the wild population.

Fun Fact: One of the unique features of the Bongo antelope is that it is one of only a few animal species in the world where horns can be found on both male and female sexes

Amur Leopard

Amur Leopard
(Panthera pardus orientalis)

Endangered Status: Critically Endangered

The Amur leopard is a leopard subspecies native to the Primorye region of southeastern Russia and the Jilin Province of northeast China. It is classified as <u>Critically Endangered</u> since 1996 by IUCN.

Amur leopards are threatened by poaching, encroaching civilization, new roads, and exploitation of forests. There are less than 70 left in the wild.

Fun Fact: Leopards can hear five times more sounds than humans, even the ultrasonic squeaks made by mice.

POLAR BEAR

POLAR BEAR
(<u>Ursus</u> <u>maritimus</u>)

Endangered Status: Vulnerable

Today, it is estimated that there are only 22,000 to 27,000 polar bears throughout the Arctic.

Risks to the polar bear include climate change, pollution in the form of toxic contaminants, conflicts with shipping, stresses from recreational polar-bear watching, and oil and gas exploration and development.

Fun Fact: Built to stay warm in their cold habitat, polar bears sometimes overheat and have to cool off in the chilly water.

California Condor

California Condor
(Gymnogyps californianus)

Endangered Status: Critically Endangered

Condor numbers dramatically declined in the 20th century due to poaching, lead poisoning, and habitat destruction.

A conservation plan was put in place by the United States government that led to the capture of all 22 remaining wild condors in 1987. These surviving birds were bred at the San Diego Zoo Safari Park and the Los Angeles Zoo. Numbers rose through captive breeding and, beginning in 1991, condors were reintroduced into the wild.

Fun Fact: With a wingspan of 10 feet and weighing up to 26 pounds, the California Condor is the largest North American land bird

Zambesi Lechwe

Zambesi Lechwe
(Kobus leche)

Endangered Status: Threatened

Originally spread across the once-vast wetlands, today, Lechwes survive mainly in and around protected areas and game reserves

Predators and hunting have caused numbers to decline, but habitat loss is the greatest threat. Lechwe are highly dependent on the specialized wetland habitats for which they are adapted, and have been eliminated from much of their former ranges as wetlands have been drained, regulated or otherwise influenced by man's activities.

Fun Fact: The hind legs are somewhat longer in proportion than in other antelopes, to ease long-distance running in marshy soil

South African Cheetah

South African Cheetah
(Acinonyx jubatus)

Endangered Status: Vulnerable

Approximately 12,400 cheetahs remain in the wild in twenty-five African countries

There are two main threats to the cheetah population. Hunting for the fur trade is the highest threat. Cheetah cubs have a high mortality rate due to predation by other carnivores, such as the lion and hyena.

Fun Fact: Cheetahs can accelerate to freeway speeds in just a few strides.

Eastern Black Rhinoceros

Eastern Black Rhinoceros
(Diceros bicornis michaeli)

Endangered Status: Critically Endangered

The eastern black rhino is distinguishable from the southern subspecies as it has a longer, leaner, and more curved horn. Its skin is also very grooved.

Once located in Ethiopia, Somalia, Tanzania, and Kenya, today they can only be found in Kenya (594 animals) and in northern Tanzania (80 animals). The population has declined 90% in the last three generations. They are threatened mainly from illegal poaching for their horns.

Fun Fact: The eastern black rhino is distinguishable from the southern subspecies as it has a longer, leaner, and more curved horn.

Ring-tailed Lemur

Ring-tailed Lemur
(Lemur catta)

Endangered Status: Endangered

The ring-tailed lemur is a large strepsirrhine primate and the most recognized lemur due to its long, black and white ringed tail. Like all lemurs it is endemic to the island of Madagascar.

Despite reproducing readily in captivity, numbering more than 2,000 individuals, the ring-tailed lemur is listed as endangered by the IUCN Red List due to habitat destruction and hunting for bush meat and the exotic pet trade.

Fun Fact: Their tails are ringed in alternating black and white transverse stripes, numbering 12 or 13 white rings and 13 or 14 black rings, and always ending in a black tip.

Hyacinth Macaw

Hyacinth Macaw

(Anodorhynchus hyacinthinus)

Endangered Status: Threatened

The hyacinth macaw is an endangered species due to the cage bird trade and habitat loss

In the event of the macaw being taken from its natural environment, a variety of factors alter their health such as inadequate hygiene conditions, feeding and overpopulation during the illegal practice of pet trade. Once captured and brought into captivity, mortality rates can become very high

Fun Fact: A macaw's tongue is dry, slightly scaly, and has a bone inside it, all of which makes it an excellent tool for breaking open and eating food

Somali Wild Ass

Somali Wild Ass
(Equus africanus somaliensis)

Endangered Status: Critically Endangered

Protected by the local government, Somali wild asses are still hunted for meat or for their fat, which is used medicinally and is believed to cure hepatitis

The Somali wild ass is the smallest of all the equids and is at critical risk, with only a few hundred left in the wild. Something as simple as a drought could be enough to wipe out the species completely

Fun Fact: In the 1500s, the Spanish brought domesticated African wild asses to the southwestern US. These animals' descendants still roam the Southwest—we know them as burros

Okapi

Okapi
(Okapia johnstoni)

Endangered Status: Endangered

The changing politics of central Africa, hunting, and the continued loss of habitat threaten the beautiful okapi

Major threats include habitat loss due to logging and human settlement. Extensive hunting for bushmeat and skin and illegal mining have also led to population declines. A threat that has emerged quite recently is the presence of illegal armed groups around protected areas, inhibiting conservation and monitoring actions

Fun Fact: Onions are the okapis' favorite treat at the San Diego Zoo and the Safari Park. They are fed onions once a week

Rothschild Giraffe

Rothschild Giraffe
(Giraffa camelopardalis rothschildi)

Endangered Status: Endangered

Rothschild's giraffe is one of the most endangered giraffe subspecies, with only a few hundred members in the wild.

The population has dropped by an alarming 80 percent in just 10 years, most likely due to poaching. They are no match for humans with guns; giraffes are shot or snared for their meat, hide, bone marrow, and tail hair

Fun Fact: A giraffe's feet are the size of a dinner plate—12 inches across

Bactrian Camel

Bactrian Camel
(Camelus bactrianus)

Endangered Status: Critically Endangered

Fewer than a thousand (around 600 individuals) are thought to survive in the wild and the population is decreasing.

The immediate threats faced by the species are all human related. Firstly, habitat loss has been high due to development for mining and industrial complexes

Fun Fact: Camels make a rumbling growl that was one of the noises used to create Chewbacca's voice in the "Star Wars" movies

Amur Tiger

Amur Tiger
(Panthera tigris altaica)

Endangered Status: Endangered

There are six subspecies of tiger living today, all highly endangered due to human hunting and encroachment on their forest habitat

For many years, tigers have been hunted for their fur and other body parts, some of which are used in native medicines. In some cultures, people hunt tigers for sport or to demonstrate their own bravery. Tiger hunting continues today because the body parts can be sold for a lot of money

Fun Fact: A tiger's confrontational roar contains energy in the infrasonic range, below human hearing. This helps the sound carry over long distances

African Lion

African Lion
(Panthera leo)

Endangered Status: Endangered

Due to many issues such as disease, hunting by humans, and loss of habitat, the population of lions in the wild is becoming very concerning to conservationists

Natural habitat for lions is now found only in protected reserves, and lion movement between prides is becoming more limited. While lion hunting is banned in many African countries, trophy hunting is still allowed in some places

Fun Fact: Lions can often survive in extreme drought conditions, eating tsama melons for moisture in the Kalahari Desert

African Elephant

African Elephant
(Loxodonta africana)

Endangered Status: Threatened

The African elephant is the largest living terrestrial animal. African elephants are found in Eastern, Southern, Central, and West Africa, in dense forests, mopane and miombo woodlands, Sahelian scrub or deserts.

The World Wildlife Foundation states that the two threats that impact African elephants the most are the demand for ivory and changes in land usage. The majority of the ivory leaving Africa continues to be acquired and transported illegally, and over 80% of all the raw ivory traded comes from poached African elephants.

Fun Fact: Unlike Asian elephants, both male and female African elephants have tusks.

Northern White Rhinoceros

Northern White Rhinoceros
(Ceratotherium simum cottoni)

Endangered Status: Critically Endangered

<u>There are **ONLY 5** of these rhinoceros left in the world!</u>

Three remain in the care of the Ol Pejeta Conservancy in Kenya, one lives at Dvur Kralove Zoo in the Czech Republic and one remains in the African plains exhibit at the San Diego Zoo Safari Park, a female named Nola.

Fun Fact: White rhinos have a hump of muscle on their neck and shoulders to hold up a head that can weigh 800 to 1,000 pounds.

NSEFU WILDLIFE CONSERVATION FOUNDATION

NSEFU Wildlife Conservation Foundation (NWCF)
A Nonprofit Organization For The Preservation And Protection Of Endangered Species.
Creating Job Opportunities Through Community Projects And Sponsoring Scholarships To Educate Local Children
NSEFU Village Is One Of The Poorest Villages In Eastern Zambia And This Foundation Benefits Their Community

HTTP://WWW.NSEFUWILDLIFE.COM

NSEFU WILDLIFE CONSERVATION FOUNDATION IS A NONPROFIT ORGANIZATION FOUNDED ON THE PRINCIPLES OF COMPASSION, ACTION, AND RESULTS.

AFRICA'S WILDLIFE IS UNDER SIEGE AT LEVELS NEVER BEFORE SEEN, AND WE ARE AT THE PRECIPICE OF LOSING THE PLANET'S MOST MAGNIFICENT AND MAJESTIC ANIMALS FOREVER. AT **NSEFU**, WE SAY "*NOT ON OUR WATCH*".

OUR MISSION STATEMENT... "**NSEFU** WILL COMBAT WILDLIFE CRIMES WITH THE GENIUS OF TECHNOLOGY AND *BOOTS-ON-THE-GROUND ACTION*." WE HAVE *PIONEERING TECHNOLOGY* THAT WILL HELP PROTECT, EDUCATE, AND PREVENT THE FURTHER DESTRUCTION OF ECOSYSTEMS THAT HAVE BEEN HIGHLY STRESSED. WE TURN ***DONATIONS INTO ACTION*** WITH WELL-THOUGHT OUT , PRINCIPLED STRATEGIES THAT INCORPORATE THE BIG PICTURE OF WILDLIFE CONSERVATION IN CONJUNCTION WITH THE LOCAL COMMUNITY. EVERYTHING WE DO WILL BE CONJUNCTION WITH LOCAL AND GOVERNMENT AUTHORITIES. IT TAKES TIME TO DO THINGS RIGHT, AND WE WANT TO DO THIS PROPERLY WITH THE BACKING OF THE GOVERNMENT. WE ARE ALL IN THIS CRITICALLY IMPORTANT FIGHT TOGETHER, AND IF WE DO THINGS IMPROPERLY...NO ONE WINS.

100 ELEPHANTS DIE **EACH DAY** TO POACHING, THERE ARE *LESS THAN 5,000 RHINOS* LEFT IN THE WILD, AND LIONS, ONCE THE KINGS OF THE JUNGLE, COUNT LESS THAN 25,000 REMAINING IN AFRICA. THIS IS ABSOLUTELY <u>UNACCEPTABLE</u> AND WE AT **NSEFU** WILL DO OUR BEST EVERYDAY IN FIGHTING THE GOOD FIGHT. PLEASE JOIN OUR FAMILY AND HELP PROTECT AFRICA'S WILDLIFE AND GIVE SPECIES WHO ARE IN THE FIGHT OF THEIR LIFE A CHANCE TO SURVIVE AND THRIVE. THAT IS WHAT WE DO AT **NSEFU**. THANK YOU FOR YOUR GENEROSITY.

ABOUT THE AUTHOR

Born in Petaluma, California during the early 1970's, Bradley Zink grew up with a passion for books. Instilled in him by his parents, and surrounded with a library of books by Dr. Seuss, Mark Twain and Charles Dickens, to name a few, he developed a true passion for reading.

After the birth of his son, Alex, and being a stay-at-home dad, he too instilled the power of reading in his son, too. Using Dr. Seuss as the building blocks for teaching him, Bradley aspired to create a book for Alex, and all children to enjoy. With his son as his muse and inspiration, Bradley is constantly testing out his writings on the world's harshest critic, his son Alex.

www.ingramcontent.com/pod-product-compliance
Lightning Source LLC
Chambersburg PA
CBHW041512280526
45792CB00004B/1223